THE
UK TO USA
DICTIONARY

BY JOHN HUNTER &

CLAUDINE DERVAES

Copyright © 1994

Claudine Dervaes and John Hunter

ISBN 0-933143-18-4

SOLITAIRE PUBLISHING
P.O. BOX 14508
TAMPA, FL 33690-4508
(813) 876-0286

Library of Congress Catalog Card Number 94-92182

TABLE OF CONTENTS

PREFACE

Of the words listed in this dictionary
some meanings are obvious, others may
cause confusion and misunderstanding
when used in the U.S. or in the U.K.

Many slang words are included. However,
their listing in this dictionary does not
encourage nor condone the use of any
derogatory or negative connotation.

Words generally used throughout Britain
and the U.S. have been chosen, as opposed
to ones that may be used in a certain
region or locale.

It is also important to note that word
<u>spellings</u> will differ. Theatre, centre
and other words ending with "re" in U.K.
are spelled with "er" in the U.S. (theater,
center). Several U.S. words having a "z"
(realize, computerize, etc.) are spelled
with an "s" in the U.K. (realise, compu-
terise).

Pronunciations will also differ. Britons may say "HOO-ston" instead of "HEW-ston," "VITT-a-min" instead of "VYE-ta-min," "SHED-yule" not "SKED-yule," "HAR-ass" instead of "har-ASS," "la-BOR-atory" versus "LAB-ratory."

The Welsh language has not been included - it is completely different and distinct.

We hope you enjoy this little handbook of all those terms from "A" to "Zed" that separate our "common language."

THE U.K. to U.S.A. DICTIONARY
by John Hunter and Claudine Dervaes

ABBREVIATIONS USED

abbr.	abbreviation
dial.	dialect
n.	noun
N. Eng.	Northern England
punc.	punctuation
Sc.	Scottish
v.	verb

UK	USA

A

A BIT OFF	somewhat annoying, unfair
ACCLIMATISED	acclimated
ACID DROP	hard candy with a bitter taste
ADVERT	advertisement/commercial
AERIAL	antenna
AERODROME/PLANE	airdrome/plane
AFTERS	dessert
AGLEY (dialect)	off the intended route/awry
"A" LEVELS	"advanced" high school exams
ANORAK	parka
APPROVED SCHOOL	juvenile detention center
ARSE	ass, buttocks
ARTICULATED LORRY	tractor trailer
AUBERGINE	eggplant
AULD LANG SYNE	the old days
AUTUMN	fall

B

BACCY	tobacco
BACK BENCHER	Member of Parliament who is not a Minister
BACK OF BEYOND	the sticks, the boonies
BAFFIES (Sc.)	slippers
BANGER	sausage

UK	USA
BANGERS AND MASH	sausages and mashed potatoes
BANG ON	just right, terrific
BANK HOLIDAY	legal holiday
BANK NOTE	bill
BANNOCK (Sc.)	unleavened oatmeal cake
BAP	hamburger bun
BARGEE	person working on a barge
BARM CAKE	hamburger bun
BARMY	crazy/silly
BARRISTER	lawyer able to appear in the upper courts
BARTON	farm yard
BATMAN	British Army Officer's Orderly
BAWBEE (dialect)	trifle/something insignificant
BEADLE	church official
BEAK	school headmaster/justice of the peace
BEANO/BEANFEAST	employer's annual dinner/ any celebration dinner
BED ONLY	hotel room without meals
BEDSIT/TER	one room apartment, sometimes including kitchen; a studio apt.
BEER & SKITTLES	pleasure, amusement
BELISHA BEACON	flashing amber light for a pedestrian crossing
BEN (Sc.)	a mountain peak
BERK/BURK	jerk
BESPOKE or MADE TO MEASURE	custom-made

2

UK	USA
BETTING SHOP	licensed public betting office
BIFFIN	red cooking apple
BIG DIPPER	roller-coaster
BILL (restaurant)	check or tab
BILL (account)	account
BILLYCOCK (N.Eng.)	derby hat
BIRO	ballpoint pen
BIRTHDAY HONOR'S LIST	list of people who have titles given to them on the sovereign's birthday
BISCUIT (sweet)	cookie
BISCUIT	cracker
BLACK OR WHITE (coffee)	without or with cream
BLACKLEG/SCAB	scab (strike breaker)
BLACK TREACLE	molasses
BLIND (window)	shade
BLINDER (TO PLAY A)	to do really well
BLOCK OF FLATS	apartment house/building
BLOKE	man or fellow
BLOOMER	mistake or blooper
BLOW THE GAFF	give away a secret/plot
BLUE-EYED BOY	fair-haired boy, favorite
BLUE FUNK	state of fright/terror
BOARD	interview, review, or promotion panel
BOB'S YOUR UNCLE	all is well
BOBBY	police officer
BOILED SWEET	hard candy

3

UK	USA
BOLLARD	traffic cone, barricade
BONCE	person's head
BONKERS	crazy
BONNET (auto)	hood
BOOK	make reservations
BOOK TOKEN	gift certificate redeemable in book shops
BOOT (auto)	trunk
BORSTAL	juvenile detention center
BOTTOM DRAWER	hope chest
BOTTOM GEAR	first gear/lowest gear
BOWLER	derby hat
BOWLS	lawn bowling
BOXING DAY	December 26
BOX ROOM	storeroom (house)
BOX SPANNER	socket wrench
BRACES	suspenders
BRACKETS (punc.)	parentheses
BRAE (Sc.)	hillside
BRAW (Sc.)	good, fine
BREAK	recess at school, work, etc.
BREEZE BLOCK	cinder block
BRIDGE ROLL	hot dog bun
BRIEF	attorney engaged by a client
BROAD BEAN	lima bean
BROLLY	umbrella
BROWNED OFF	fed up, bored
BROWN STUDY (IN A)	daydreaming
BUBBLE & SQUEAK	cold meat fried with cabbage and potatoes

4

UK	USA
BUCKSHEE	something free/a gift
BUILDING SOCIETY	organization providing loans (especially for house purchases) and investment accounts
BULLY BEEF	corned beef
BUMF	paperwork/toilet paper
BUNFIGHT	tea party
BUNS	muffins/cupcakes
BURGLE	burglarize
BURN (Sc.)	small stream or brook
BUSBY/BEARSKIN	guardsman's tall fur hat
BUT AND BEN (Sc.)	two roomed cottage
BUTTONHOLE	boutonniere
BUTTONS	bellboy
BUTTY	sandwich
BYRE	cowshed

C

UK	USA
C.V. (Curriculum Vitae)	resume
CABOOSE	ship's galley
CAKES AND ALE	the good things of life
CALL BOX	phone booth
CALLOVER (betting)	announcing the latest odds
CANDY FLOSS	cotton candy
CANNON (billiards)	carom
CANTEEN OF CUTLERY	boxed set of cutlery

5

UK	USA
CAP (sports)	special hat awarded to members of international sports teams
CAPSTAN LATHE	turret lathe
CARAVAN	trailer (recreational)
CARAVANETTE	small R.V. (recreational vehicle)
CAR BOOT SALE	temporary flea market where goods are displayed on car trunks
CAREER (vehicle out of control)	careen
CARETAKER/PORTER	janitor
CAR PARK	parking lot
CARRIAGE PAID	free shipping
CARRIAGEWAY	highway
CASTER SUGAR	white, finely granulated sugar
CATAPULT	slingshot
CATHERINE WHEEL	pinwheel firework
CAT'S EYES	reflectors on roads
CATTLE GRID	Texas gate, cattle guard
CENTRAL RESERVATION	median
CHAR (cup of)	tea
CHARABANC	tour bus/motorcoach
CHARLADY	housemaid/cleaning maid
CHASE	unenclosed tract of land
CHEAP AND NASTY	low cost and poor quality
CHEERIO	goodbye
CHEESED OFF	bored, exasperated
CHEMIST	pharmacist

6

UK	USA
CHEMIST SHOP	pharmacy/drugstore
CHEST OF DRAWERS	dresser
CHIP BOARD	particle board
CHIPS	french fries
CHIROPODIST	podiatrist
CHIVVY	to chase/to hurry up
CHOCK A BLOCK	jammed or crowded
CHOCOLATE/SWEETS	candy
CHORLEY CAKE	small round pastry filled with sultanas
CHUFFED	pleased
CIDER	alcoholic cider/hard cider
CINEMA	movie house/theater
CITY CENTRE	downtown
CITY EDITOR	newspaper editor of business/finance
CLASS/FORM (school)	grade
CLEARWAY	road where stopping is prohibited
CLERK OF WORKS	construction overseer
CLIPPIE	woman collecting fares on buses, etc.
CLOAKROOM	checkroom
CLOAKROOM ATTENDANT	hat/coat check person
CLOBBER	clothing
CLOTH CAP	blue collar worker
CLOTHESPEG	clothespin
CLOUGH	narrow valley
COARSE FISH/ING	fresh water fish/fishing, excluding salmon and trout

UK	USA
COB	round crisp loaf of bread
COBBLERS	nonsense, bunk
COCK-A-HOOP	elated
COCK A SNOOK	to thumb one's nose
COCK-UP	mistake or blooper
CODLING	a cooking apple
CODSWALLOP	gibberish/nonsense
COLLAR STIFFENER AND STUD	collar stay and button
COLLIERY	coal mine with buildings
COMBS. (abbr. for combinations)	combined underwear, longjohns
COMMERCIAL TRAVELER	traveling sales representative
COMMISSIONAIRE	uniformed door person at theaters, etc.
COMMUNICATION CORD	emergency handle
COMPERE	show host/master of ceremonies
CONKERS	game played with horse chestnuts on strings
CONSCRIPT	draftee
CONSCRIPTION	the draft
CONSTABLE	police officer
CONSTABULARY	police force
COOKER	stove/range
COOK THE BOOKS	falsify records
CORACLE	small wickerwork boat
CORN FLOUR	cornstarch
CORPORATION	city government
COSH	blackjack/bludgeon
COS LETTUCE	romaine lettuce

UK	USA
COSTERMONGER	street seller of fruits, fish, etc.
COT	babybed/crib
COTTAGE LOAF	loaf of bread made from two pieces, a smaller one on top of a larger one
COTTON REEL	thread spool
COTTON WOOL	cotton balls/cotton pads/absorbent cotton
COURGETTE	zucchini
COURIER	tour escort, tour conductor
COURT SHOES	pumps
COWSLIP	marsh marigold
CRANE FLY	daddy longlegs, harvestman
CREAM CRACKER	soda cracker
CRECHE/NURSERY	day care facility
CRISPS	chips (potato)
CROWD PULLER	drawing card/draw
CRUMPET	English muffin
CRY OFF	beg off
CUDDY (Sc.)	donkey
CULVER	pigeon/dove
CUPBOARD	closet
CUPPA	cup of tea
CUPS (IN ONE'S)	while drunk
CURRENT ACCOUNT	checking account
CUTE	ingenious, clever, attractive
CUT THROAT RAZOR	straight razor

D

UK	USA
DARBIES	handcuffs
DARBY AND JOAN CLUB	club for the elderly
DAVENPORT	writing desk, bureau
DEAR	expensive
DEASIL (Sc.)	clockwise
DEATH DUTY	inheritance tax
DECOKE (auto)	head/valve job
DEMOB.	military discharge
DEPOSIT ACCOUNT	savings account
DESICCATED (coconut)	shredded
DIAMANTE	rhinestone
DICEY/DODGY	problematic/risky
DICKEY SEAT	rumble seat
DIGS	lodgings
DINNER HOUR	lunch break
DINNER LADY (school)	cafeteria lady
DIP	switch vehicle's lights to low beam
DISTRICT	precinct
DIVER (ornithology)	loon
DIVERSION	detour
DOCH AND DORRIS (WEE) (Sc.)	drink before leaving, one for the road
DOCKET	label listing package contents

UK	USA
DOING A BOMB	successful
DOLE (THE)	unemployment benefit from the state
DONKEY'S YEARS	dog's age
DOSS HOUSE	cheap lodging, flop house
DOUBLE (billiards)	bank shot
DRAPERS	fabric store
DRAUGHT EXCLUDER	weather stripping
DRAUGHTS	checkers
DRAWING PIN	thumbtack
DRESS CIRCLE	mezzanine/loge
DRESSING GOWN	bathrobe
DROP A BRICK	be indiscreet
DROP A CLANGER	make a big mistake
DUCK ('S EGG)	out without scoring at cricket
DUAL CARRIAGEWAY	divided highway
DUFF GEN	bum steer
DUMMY (child's)	pacifier
DUSTBIN	trash can
DUSTCART	garbage truck
DUSTMAN	garbageworker/sanitary engineer
DUSTY (NOT SO)	fairly good
DUTCH CAP	birth control diaphragm

E

UK	USA
EACH WAY BET	win or place
EARTH/EARTHWIRE (electrical)	ground/groundwire

UK	USA
ECCLES CAKE	round pastry cake filled with currants
EIDERDOWN	comforter
ELDRITCH (Sc.)	weird, hideous
EMULSION PAINT	flat paint
ENGAGED (phone)	busy
ENTREE	meal before the main course
ESQ./ESQUIRE (example: J. Smith, Esq.)	title for a man when Mr. is not used
ESTATE AGENT	realtor
ESTATE CAR, SHOOTING BRAKE	station wagon

F

UK	USA
FACE FLANNEL	washcloth
FAG	cigarette
FASH (Sc.)	trouble, bother, inconvenience
FATHER CHRISTMAS	Santa Claus
FEEDER	child's bib/bottle
FELL	mountain, hill, high moorland
FILLING STATION	gas station
FILM	movie
FIRE BRIGADE	fire department
FIRST FLOOR	second floor
FISH MONGER	dealer in fish
FISH SLICE	spatula

12

UK	USA
FITTED CARPET	wall to wall carpet
FIVES	handball
FIXTURES (sports)	schedule
FLAG DAY	tag day
FLAT	apartment
FLEX	electric cord
FLICK KNIFE	switchblade
FLIT (Sc.)	move house
FLUID OUNCE (U.K.)	0.9606 U.S. fluid ounces
FLUTTER	small bet
FLY	alert, astute
FLYOVER	overpass
FOOTBALL	soccer
FORCE	small waterfall
FORTNIGHT	two weeks
FRANKING MACHINE	postage meter
FREE HOUSE, FREE OFF LICENCE	pub, liquor store not tied to a brewery
FRIGATE (ship)	small destroyer
FROWSTY	musty, stale smelling
FRUIT MACHINE	slot machine
FUBSY	fat, squat
FULL STOP (punc.)	period
FUNNY BONE	crazy bone

G

UK	USA
GAFFER	foreman, old man
GALLERY	balcony
GALLON (U.K.)	1.2 U.S. gallons
GAMMY (leg)	slightly lame
GAMP	large umbrella
GANGWAY	aisle
GAOL/GAOLER	jail/jailer
GARDEN	yard
GARTH	paddock, close
GASH	spare, extra
GAZUMP	raise the agreed price of a house after receiving a better offer
GEAR LEVER	gear stick, stick shift
GEN	information
GET KNOTTED	stop annoying me
GET THE HUMP	become irritated, sulk
GET THE PUSH	to be fired, sacked
GEYSER (gas)	water heater
GILL, GHYLL	mountain torrent, ravine
GLEN (Sc.)	narrow valley
GOBBET	small amount
GOB STOPPER	jaw breaker
GO FOR A BURTON	lost, destroyed, killed
GOODS/GOODS WAGON	freight/freight truck
GORBLIMEY/BLIMEY	expression of surprise or indignation

UK	USA
GORMLESS	stupid, lacking sense
GO SLOW	worker's slow down
GO SPARE	become very annoyed
GRADELY	excellent, handsome
GRAMMAR SCHOOL	high school
GREAT COAT	military overcoat
GREENFLY	green aphid, plant louse
GREENGROCER	retailer of fruit and vegetables
GREEN PEPPER	bell pepper
GREET (Sc.)	weep, cry
GRIFF	news, reliable information
GRILL	broil
GRIZZLE	whine, sob
GROUND FLOOR	first floor
GROUNDAGE	port taxes
GUARD (train)	conductor
GUARD'S VAN (train)	caboose
GUBBINS	gadgets, useless items
GUDGEON PIN	wrist pin
GUY (FAWKES)	effigy of Guy Fawkes burnt on November 5
GYMKHANA	competition for horse riding and jumping
GYP (GIVE SOMEONE)	torment, treat unmercifully

H

UK	USA
HABERDASHERY	notions store
HAIR GRIP	bobby pin
HAIR SLIDE	barette
HALF-TERM (holiday)	semester/term break
HALT	a way station, whistle-stop
HANDBAG	purse
HAND OFF (rugby)	push away opponent with palm of hand
HANGER	wooded area on a steep, sloping hill
HA'P'ORTH (half-penny worth)	slightest, minute quantity
HARD BAKED/BOILED	cynical, disillusioned
HARDCORE	broken bricks and rocks used for road foundations
HARD LINES	bad luck
HARD SHOULDER	emergency lane
HARL (Sc.)	drag along the ground
HAVER	talk foolishly, babble, hesitate
HEADMASTER/MISTRESS	principal
HEATH	open land, covered with low shrubs, usually heather
HEATH ROBINSON	absurdly ingenious and impractical
HELTER-SKELTER	corkscrew slide
HIDE	blind (hunting or observing)

UK	USA
HIGH TEA	evening meal
HIRE PURCHASE	installment plan
HOARDING	billboard, signboard
HOCKEY	field hockey
HOGMANAY (Sc.)	New Year's Eve Celebration
HOLIDAY	vacation
HOLME	land around river that is subject to flooding
HOMELY (person)	pleasant and unpretentious
HOOTER	horn, siren
HOOTER	nose
HOUSING ESTATE	subdivision
HUM	unpleasant smell
HUMBUG	minty, hard-boiled candy
HUNDREDWEIGHT	112 pounds
HUNDREDS AND THOUSANDS	nonpareil

I

ICED LOLLY	popsicle
ICING SUGAR	powdered/confectioner's sugar
IDENTIFICATION PARADE	line up
IMMERSION HEATER	electric water heater
INCH	small Scottish island
INFANT SCHOOL	school for those age 5-7

UK	USA
INGLE	fire burning in hearth
INGLE NOOK	corner by a fireplace
INJECTION	shot
INLAND REVENUE	internal revenue
INTAKE	batch of recruits
INTERIOR SPRUNG	innerspring
INTERVAL	intermission
INVERTED COMMAS	quotation marks
INVIGILATOR	proctor
IRONMONGER	hardware store

J

JAB	shot
JANNOCK (dialect)	honest, genuine
JEMMY	jimmy
JERRY	chamber pot
JIGGERY POKERY	underhand scheming
JOBATION	a lengthy reprimand
JOCK	Scottish person
JOE BLOGGS	John Doe
JOINT OF MEAT	roast
JOSSER	fellow
JUDDER (mechanical)	vibrate or shake violently
JUG	pitcher
JUGGED HARE	rabbit stew

18

UK	USA
JUGGERNAUT	very large and heavy truck
JUMBLE SALE	used goods collected and sold, usually for charity
JUMPER	pullover, sweater
JUNCTION (ROAD)	intersection
JUNIOR SCHOOL	school for ages 7-11

K

KEEP YOUR PECKER UP	maintain your courage
KEN (Sc.)	know, be acquainted with
KENSPECKLE	conspicuous
KERB	curb (edge of road)
KERFUFFLE	fuss, commotion
KICK ONE'S HEELS	to wait around
KILLNER JAR	ball/mason jar
KIOSK (phone)	booth
KIOSK (news)	stand
KIPPER	smoked herring
KIRBY GRIP	bobby pin
KIRK (Sc.)	church
KISSING GATE	gate allowing people through but not livestock
KIT (sports)	uniform
KIT BAG	soldier's duffel bag
KITE MARK	official mark indicating goods approved by British Standard Institution

UK	USA
KNACKERED	tired, worn-out
KNACKER'S YARD	place where old horses are slaughtered
KNEES UP	lively dance party
KNICKERS	women's panties
KNOCKING SHOP	brothel
KNOCK UP	wake up

L

L PLATE	plate on a vehicle indicating student driver
LABEL	tag
LADDER (hosiery)	run
LADYBIRD	ladybug
LARDER	pantry
LASHINGS	plenty, an abundance
LAST POST	taps
LAY ABOUT	loafer
LAY BY	designated places for vehicles to pull over
LEAD	leash
LEADER/LEADING ARTICLE	main editorial/commentary
LEADER (orchestra)	concertmaster
LEATHERJACKET	harvestman grub

UK	USA
LEFT LUGGAGE	baggage room
LET	lease, rent
LETTER BOX	mailbox
LEVANT	to abscond with debt unpaid
LEVEL CROSSING	grade/railroad crossing
LIBERTY BOAT	boat carrying sailors ashore on leave
LIBERTY BODICE	closefitting women's undergarment
LICENSED VICTUALLER	innkeeper with a liquor license
LIFT	elevator
LIGHTING UP TIME	time when cars must switch on headlights
LIMITED/LTD.	Incorporated/Inc.
LIP SALVE	chapstick
LIQUID PARAFFIN	odorless, tasteless, mild laxative
LIVER SAUSAGE	liverwurst
LOCAL (THE)	tavern, neighborhood pub
LOCH (Sc.)	lake
LOCK UP	shop or garage (without living quarters)
LODGER	boarder
LOLLIPOP LADY/MAN	school crossing guard
LOLLOP	ungainly walk
LONG CHALK (BY A)	by a long shot, by far
LOO	bathroom, restroom
LOOSE COVER	slip cover
LORD MUCK	high-muck-a-muck

UK	USA
LORRY	truck, vehicle for carrying large goods
LOSE MARKS	count off
LOUD HAILER	bull horn
LOUNGE SUIT	business suit
LUCERNE	alfalfa/fodder
LUCKY DIP	grab bag
LUM (Sc.)	chimney
LUNCHEON VOUCHER	given to employees as part of pay and exchangeable for meals at many restaurants
LURCHER	a cross between a sheep dog and a greyhound
LUTINE BELL	bell rung at Lloyd's of London to announce the loss of a ship

M

MAC, MACK	mackintosh coat
MADEIRA CAKE	rich, sweet sponge cake
MAINS LEAD	outlet plug, adaptor
MARCHING ORDERS	walking papers, dismissal
MARKET GARDEN	truck farm
MARRAM GRASS	dune grass
MARROW (vegetable)	squash
MATCH (soccer)	game
MATE	buddy

UK	USA
MATELOT	sailor
MAUNDY MONEY	specially minted silver coins distributed by the reigning monarch to the poor on Maundy Thursday
MERCER	dealer in textiles, e.g., silks
MERRY DANCERS	Aurora Borealis
METHS (see below)	
METHYLATED SPIRITS	denatured alcohol
MEWS	courtyard stables, often converted into dwellings
MILK FLOAT	light truck (usually electric) for delivering milk
MINCED MEAT/BEEF	hamburger meat, ground beef
MINCER	meat grinder
"MIND YOUR P'S AND Q'S"	"Be careful to be polite"
MIZZLE	to run away
MOGGIE	cat
MOIDER/MOITHER	confuse, worry, pester
MOKE	donkey
MONEY FOR JAM/OLD ROPE	profit for little effort
MOT (MINISTRY OF TRANSPORT) TEST	road safety test for vehicles
MOTHER'S DAY	fourth Sunday in Lent
MOTORWAY	freeway
MRS. MOP	cleaning woman/housemaid
MUD GUARD	fender
MUG	gullible person

N

UK	USA
NAAFI	PX
NANCY/NANCY BOY	effeminate male/homosexual
NANNY	child's nurse
NAPPER	head
NAPPY	diaper
NARK (COPPER'S)	informer (police), stool pigeon
NARK	to annoy, make angry
NATIONAL TRUST	historic and natural beauty preservation organization
NATTER	talk, grumble
NAVVY	laborer on roads, railway
NEARSIDE (vehicle)	passenger side
NEAT (drink)	straight
NEB	bill, beak, tip
NEEDLE MATCH	rival match
NEEP (Sc.)	turnip
NET CURTAINS	sheer curtains, under-drapes
NEVER NEVER (THE)	installment plan
NEWMARKET (card game)	Michigan
NEWSAGENT	newsdealer/newstand
NICKER	one pound sterling
NIFF	a smell/stink
NIL	no score, zip
999	911
NINETEEN TO THE DOZEN	rapidly, very quickly

UK	USA
NIPPER	young boy or girl
NIPPY	agile, nimble, swift
NOB	person of wealth or high social position
NOBBLE	tamper with racehorse to prevent its winning
NOG	strong beer
NOSH	food (n.)/eat (v.)
NOSH UP	feast, large meal
NOT A FULL SHILLING	mentally deficient
NOT HALF	very much
NOTICE BOARD	bulletin board
NOT ON YOUR NELLY	no way/certainly not
NOUGHT	zero
NOUGHTS & CROSSES	tick-tack-toe
NUMBER PLATE	license plate
NURSING HOME	private hospital

O

"O" LEVELS	"ordinary" high school exams
O.A.P. (Old Age Pensioner)	senior citizen
OFF COLOUR	feeling ill
OFF LICENCE	liquor store
OFF PUTTING	disconcerting, repellent
OFF SIDE (vehicle)	driver's side
OFF THE PEG	off the rack

UK	USA
OFF THE RAILS	acting strangely or irresponsibly
OLD BILL	police
OLD BOY	alumnus
OLD LAG	hardened criminal
OLD SCHOOL TIE	upper class solidarity
OLD SWEAT	experienced person, old soldier
O.N.O (OR NEAR OFFER)	O.B.O. (or best offer)
ON THE MIKE	idling, being lazy
OPERATING THEATRE	operating room
OPPO	friend, colleague
OPPOSITION (THE)	main parliamentary party not in office
OPTIC	measuring device attached to liquor/wine bottle necks
ORBITAL	beltway
ORRA (Sc.)	extra, odd
OUTSIDE BROADCAST	broadcast on location
OVEN CLOTH/GLOVES	potholders/gloves
OVERTAKE	pass
OXTER (Sc.)	armpit

P

UK	USA
P.A.Y.E. (PAY AS YOU EARN)	income tax deducted from salary
PACK (of cards)	deck
PACK UP	stop working, break down
PADDY	tantrum, fit
PANDA CAR	police patrol car
PANTECHNICON	furniture removal van
PANTOMIME (PANTO)	Christmas show with singing, dancing, and slapstick comedy, usually with audience participation and normally adapted from fairy tales.
PANTS/UNDERPANTS	men's underwear
PARAFFIN	kerosene
PARALYTIC	very drunk
PARCEL	package
PARKY	chilly (weather)
PASS OUT (military)	finish training
PASTY	crusted pie
PATCH (GOOD OR BAD)	period, stage
PAVEMENT	sidewalk
PAWKY (Sc.)	shrewd, having a dry humor
PAY PACKET	pay envelope
PECKISH	slightly hungry
PELICAN CROSSING	pedestrian crossing with lights
PELMET	valance
PENNY DREADFUL	cheap storybook or magazine
PEPPER POT	pepper shaker

UK	USA
PERMANENT WAY	rail or tram tracks
PERRY	hard cider made from pears
PETROL	gasoline, gas
PETROL BOMB	Molotov cocktail
PICTURES	movies
PIGEON PAIR	boy and girl twins
PILLAR BOX	mailbox, mail drop
PINK	young salmon
PIP (THE)	depressed, annoyed
PITCH (sports)	field
PLANT (billiards)	combination shot
PLASTER	band aid
PLIMSOLLS/PUMPS	canvas sports shoes, Keds
PLOUGHMAN'S LUNCH	meal of bread, cheese, etc.
PLUS-FOURS/TWOS	knickers/knickerbockers
PO-FACED	solemn, humorless
POINT DUTY	traffic duty
POLICE INSPECTOR	police captain
POLONECK (sweater)	turtleneck
POLONY	bologna
POMFRET/PONTEFRACT CAKE	small, flat, round licorice candy
PONCE	pimp; to move about effeminately
PONTOON (cards)	blackjack, 21
PONY	twenty-five pounds sterling
POOFTER	male homosexual, effeminate man
POP	hock, pawn

UK	USA
POPPET	small dainty person, term of endearment
POSITIVE DISCRIMINATION	affirmative action
POST	mail
POSTAGE	shipping
POSTAL CODE	zip code
POSTAL ORDER	money order
POSY	small bunch of flowers
POT HOLER	spelunker, cave explorer
POTTED MEAT	head cheese
POTTY	silly, slightly crazy
POWER POINT	electrical outlet
PRAM (PERAMBULATOR)	baby carriage
PRANG	crash (vehicle)
PREFECT (school)	student monitor
PREP	school homework
PRESS MARK (library)	call number
PRESS STUDS/POPPERS	snaps
PRIVATE PATIENT	patient not under the National Health Service
PRIVY PURSE	the monarchy's allowance
PROM	concert
PUBLICAN	manager/owner of a tavern
PUBLIC CONVENIENCE	public restroom/toilets
PUBLIC SCHOOL	private school
PUDDING	dessert
PUNCH UP	fight or brawl
PUNNET	small basket for fruit

UK	USA
PUNTER	customer, specifically of a prostitute; also a gambler
PURCHASE TAX	sales tax
PURLER	fall head first
PURSE	change purse, coin purse
PUSH CHAIR	stroller
PUT A SOCK IN IT	shut up, be quiet
PUTTY MEDAL	fit reward for small service

Q

UK	USA
QUARENDEN	red apple
QUARTER DAYS	Mar. 25, Jun. 24, Sep. 29, and Dec. 25
QUARTER-LIGHT (vehicle)	wing window
QUAVER	an eighth note
QUEER ONE'S PITCH	upset one's plans
QUEUE	a line
QUEUE UP	stand in line
QUEUE JUMP	cut in line
QUID	one pound sterling
QUIDS IN	made a profit
QUIFF	curl of hair over the forehead

UK	USA

R

RACHMANISM	landlord's exploitation of slum tenants
RAG	prank
RAG AND BONE MAN	itinerant dealer in old clothes and other goods, junkman
RAG DAY	annual comic day held by students to raise money for charity
RAMP	swindle, usually by overcharging
RASHER (bacon)	slice
RATES	local utility charges
RATING	non-commissioned sailor
RAWLPLUGS	anchors
RECORDED DELIVERY	certified mail
RED CAP	military policeman
REDUNDANT (MADE)	laid off work, riffed
REGISTRY OFFICE	local government office which conducts marriages
REMEMBRANCE DAY	Veteran's Day
REMAND CENTRE	detention center
RETURN (ticket)	round trip
RETURNING OFFICER	official who announces election results
REVERSE CHARGES	call collect
RHINE	a large open ditch
RHINO	money, cash
RICK (neck or back)	sprain, twist
RING, RING UP	call
RING ROAD	belt highway

UK	USA
ROCKET	reprimand
ROLLER BLIND	window shade
RORTY	enjoyable
ROTA	roster
ROTOVATOR	power driven soil tiller
ROUNDABOUT	traffic circle; also a merry-go-round
ROUNDERS	game similar to baseball
ROUND TRIP	circular journey
ROUP	sell at auction
ROWAN TREE	mountain ash
RUBBER	eraser
RUBBISH TIP	trash dump
RUGGER	rugby
RUM (person)	odd, strange
RUNNER BEAN	string bean
RUNDALE/RUNRIG	joint occupation of land
RUN TO	afford
RUN UP	prelude

S

UK	USA
SAIL CLOSE TO THE WIND	almost get into trouble
SALOON CAR	sedan
SALT CELLAR	salt shaker
SAND MARTIN	bank swallow

UK	USA
SANITARY TOWEL	sanitary napkin/pad
SAPPER	soldier with the Royal Engineers
SARNIE	sandwich
SASSENACH	Scot's term for English person
SAUSAGE ROLL	sausage meat wrapped in flaky pastry
SCARPER	to run away
SCATTY	harebrained
SCOTCH EGG	hard boiled egg covered in sausage meat
SCOUSE	native of Liverpool or the Liverpudlian dialect
SCRIMSHANK	to shirk duty
SCUNNER	to feel sick; a strong dislike
SCUPPER	sink a ship, spoil plans
SECATEURS	pruning shears/clippers
SELLOTAPE	Scotch tape
SEMIBREVE	whole note
SEMI-DETACHED	duplex
SEMIQUAVER	sixteenth note
SEMOLINA	cream of wheat
SEND UP	satirize, ridicule by mimicking
SERVIETTE	table napkin
SHAW	small wood, thicket
SHIELING (Sc.)	hut used by shepherds/sportsmen
SHIPPON	cattle shed
SHOOTING BRAKE	station wagon
SHOOT THE MOON	move house at night to avoid paying rent
SHOPPING PRECINCT	shopping mall
SHORT	cocktail

33

UK	USA
SHORT LIST	list of final choices
SHOWER	contemptible or unpleasant person(s)
SHUFTI	a look (at a thing)
SIGNAL BOX (rail)	signal tower
SILENCER (auto)	muffler
SILLER (Sc.)	money
SILVER SIDE	cut of beef
SIMNEL CAKE	rich fruit cake
SINGLE	one way ticket
SINGLET	sleeveless undershirt
SISTER (WARD)	senior nurse
SKELP	hit, beat, spank
SKILLY	thin soup
SKIP	dumpster
SKIRTING BOARD	baseboard
SKIVE	avoid work
SKIVVY	a female domestic servant
SLAP & TICKLE	boisterous, amorous amusement
SLATE	criticize severely
SLEEPERS	railroad ties
SLEEPING PARTNER	silent partner
SLEEPING POLICEMEN	speed bumps
SLIP ROAD	ramp
SLOSH	to hit
SLOSHED	drunk, smashed
SMALLS	underwear
SNAFFLE	to steal
SNECK	door latch
SOLICITOR	lawyer, attorney

34

UK	USA
SONSY (Sc.)	cheerful; buxom
SPANNER	wrench
SPECIAL CONSTABLE	part-time policeman
SPEECH DAY	annual prize giving day
SPINNEY	small wood
SPIV	con man
SPONGE BAG	toiletries bag
SPOTTED DICK	plum duff
SQUADDY	private soldier, recruit
STALLS	orchestra seats
STANDARD LAMP	floor lamp
STANDING ORDER	direct/preauthorized debit
STANNARY	tin mine
STARKERS	completely naked
STARTERS	appetizers
STONE (weight)	fourteen pounds
STRATH (Sc.)	wide valley
STROPPY	bad tempered, awkward
STUMER	worthless money, fraud
STUMP UP	pay up
SUBTOPIA	urban sprawl
SUBWAY	underground pedestrian walkway
SUMP (auto)	oil pan
SUN BLIND	window awning
SURGERY (doctor's)	office (doctor's or dentist's)
SURGICAL SPIRITS	rubbing alcohol
SUS OUT	figure out; check over
SUSPENDERS	garters
SUSPENDER BELT	garter belt
SWALLOW DIVE	swan dive
SWEDE	rutabaga

UK	USA
SWEET	dessert; a candy
SWEET SHOP	candy store
SWINE FEVER	hog cholera
SWINGS AND ROUNDABOUTS	break even; "six of one, half a dozen of the other"
SWING THE LEAD	malinger
SWIPES	inferior beer
SWISS ROLL	jelly roll
SWITCHBACK	roller coaster; road with alternating ups and downs
SWIZZ	to cheat, swindle
SWOT	study in depth for exams

T

TA	thank you
TABLE	submit for discussion, propose
TAIL BACK (traffic)	back up
TANNOY	public address system
TAP	faucet
TAXI RANK	taxi stand
TEA CAKE	sweet bun with raisins
TEA TOWEL	dish towel, kitchen towel
TEDDY BOY	a youth preferring the Edwardian style of dress (a 1950's fad)
TELLY	television

36

UK	USA
TENTER	person who looks after things; watchdog
THWAITE	piece of wild land made arable
TICK	credit
TICK	a check mark
TICKETY BOO	all right, hunky dory
TICK OVER (vehicle)	idling speed
TICK TACK	manual signaling used by race course bookmakers
TIED COTTAGE	occupied by tenant only while working for the owner
TIED HOUSE	pub only allowed to sell a particular brewer's liquor
TIGHTS	panty hose
TIME TABLE	schedule
TIP LORRY	dump truck
TITCH	small person
TITFER	hat
TOFF	upper class man, a dandy
TOFFEE NOSED	snobbish, pretentious
TOMMY	a British soldier
TON	speed of 100 m.p.h.; score of 100
TOP DRAWER	of the highest social position
TOP HOLE	first rate
TOPPING	excellent
TOP UP (drink)	refill
TORCH	flashlight
TOT	jigger
TOWPATH	path alongside a river/canal

UK	USA
TRAFFIC WARDEN	parking meter patrol person, sometimes assists police in traffic duty
TRAILER (film)	preview (movie)
TRAM	streetcar
TRANSPORT CAFE	truck stop
TRAVELLING RUG	lap robe, lap blanket
TREACLE (BLACK)	molasses
TRIFLE	a dessert of sponge cake, fruit, wine, jello, custard, cream
TRILBY	fedora
TRIPPER	vacationer (especially for a day)
TRUG	shallow, wooden garden basket
TRUNCHEON	night stick
TRUNK ROAD	main highway
TUBE	subway
TUCK IN	eat heartily
TUCK SHOP	candy store (usually at a school)
TURF ACCOUNTANT	bookie
TURN UPS	pant cuffs
TUPPENNY HA'PENNY	unimportant, worthless, two bit
TWEE	dainty, quaint
TWICER	double dealer, cheat
TYKE	Yorkshireman; a rascal

UK	USA

U

UNIT TRUST	Municipal Investment Trust
UPPER CIRCLE	first balcony

V

VACUUM FLASK	Thermos
VERGER	church official
VEST	undershirt
VET	to examine and check for accuracy or suitability

W

WAD	sandwich
WAFFLE	to speak or write imprecisely
WAG	to be truant, to play hookey
WAISTCOAT	vest
WALTZER (ride)	tilt a whirl
WARDER	prison guard
WASH UP	clean dishes, etc.
WELLIES	Wellington boots
WELSH DRESSER	hutch
WENDY HOUSE	child's playhouse

39

UK	USA
WHACKED	tired out
WHIP ROUND	collection of money from a group of people
WIDE BOY	quick witted but dishonest person
WINCEYETTE	type of lightweight flannelette
WIND CHEATER	wind breaker
WINDLESTRAW	old dry grass
WINE GUM	gum drop
WINKLE-PICKERS	long, very pointed shoes
WITTER ON	speak at length about trivial matters
WONKY	shaky, unreliable
WOTCHER?	how are you?
WREN (Women's Navy)	WAVE
WRITE OFF (vehicle)	to completely wreck, total
WYND (Sc.)	alley, narrow street

Y

UK	USA
YANKEE (betting)	bet on four or more horses to win or place in different races
YOB	lout, hooligan

UK	USA

Z

ZEBRA CROSSING	pedestrian crossing
ZED	z

NOTES

USA	UK

A

A LA MODE	served with ice cream
ABSORBENT COTTON	cotton wool
ACCLIMATED	acclimatised
AFFIRMATIVE ACTION	positive discrimination
AIRDROME/PLANE	aerodrome/plane
ALUMNI/AE	former pupils
	(male/female)
ALUMNUS	old boy
AMBULANCE CHASER	lawyer who encourages
	clients to sue for
	damages after an accident
ANCHORS	rawlplugs
ANTENNA	aerial
APARTMENT	flat
APARTMENT BUILDING	block of flats
APPETIZER	starter
ARROYO	stream, gully
ASHCAN	dustbin
ASS	backside, arse

B

BALL JAR	Killner jar
BALLPARK	baseball ground

USA	UK
BALLPARK FIGURE	estimate, approximate amount
BANGS	hair fringe
BANG UP	first class, terrific
BANK SHOT (billiards)	double
BARETTE	hair slide
BARF	vomit
BARKEEP	bar tender
BASEBOARD	skirting board
BAZOO	mouth
BEAN COUNTER	accountant
BELLHOP/BELLPERSON	page
BELL PEPPER	green pepper
BELT HIGHWAY	ring road
BENNY	overcoat
BILK	swindle
BILL	banknote
BILLBOARD	hoarding
BILLFOLD	wallet
BISCUIT	a soft unsweetened roll
BITTERSWEET CHOCOLATE	plain chocolate
BLACKJACK	cosh
BLEACHERS	grandstand seats, usually unsheltered
BLIND	hide (observation)
BLOOPER	blunder, usually in public
BLUE LAWS	Sunday trading laws
BOARDWALK	raised walkway, usually by the beach

44

USA	UK
BOBBY PIN	hair grip, kirby grip
BOLOGNA	polony
BOMB	a failure, disaster
BOOKMOBILE	mobile library
BOONDOCKS/BOONIES	isolated countryside
BOONDOGGLE	trivial or unnecessary work
BOXCAR (rail)	enclosed goods wagon
BRIEFS	men's underpants
BROIL	grill
BRONX CHEER	blow a raspberry
BULL HORN	loud hailer
BULL PEN	baseball pitcher's practice area
BUMMER (slang)	unpleasant experience
BUNCO/BUNKO	swindle
BUNS/BUTT (slang)	bum, buttocks
BURGLARIZE	burgle
BURRO	small donkey
BUSBOY/BUSPERSON	waiter's assistant
BUSINESS SUIT	lounge suit
BUSS	kiss
BUSY (phone)	engaged (line)
BUTTE	solitary hill or mountain
BUTTONWOOD/SYCAMORE TREE	plane tree

C

USA	UK
CABANA	beach shelter
CABOOSE (rail)	guard's van
CALABOOSE	prison
CALL (phone)	ring
CALL COLLECT	reverse charges
CALL NUMBER (library)	press mark
CANDY	sweets, chocolate
CANDY STORE	sweet shop
CAREEN	career
CAR HOP	waiter at a drive-in restaurant
CARNIVAL	fun fair
CATERCORNER/ CATTYCORNER	diagonally opposite
CERTIFIED MAIL	recorded delivery
CHANGE/COIN PURSE	purse
CHAPSTICK	lip salve
CHARLEY HORSE	cramps (arms, legs)
CHECK (mark)	tick
CHECK (payment)	cheque
CHECK (restaurant)	bill
CHECKERS	draughts
CHECKROOM	cloakroom
CHICKADEE	titmouse
CHINCHBUG	small insect that destroys grain, etc.
CHIPPER	cheerful

46

USA	UK
CHIPS (potato)	crisps
CHOWDER	fish stew or soup
CINDER BLOCK	breeze block
CITY EDITOR	editor dealing with local news
CITY GOVERNMENT	corporation
CLOSET	cupboard
CLOSET (clothes)	wardrobe
CLOTHESPIN	clothes-peg
COLLAR, STAY AND BUTTON	collar, stiffener and stud
COMBINATION SHOT (billiards)	plant
COMFORTER	eiderdown
COMMERCIALS	adverts
CONDOMINIUM/CONDO	privately owned or leased flat
CONDUCTOR (rail)	guard
CONFECTIONER'S SUGAR	icing sugar
CONNECT (phone)	put through
CONNIPTION (fit)	a fit of rage or hysteria, "throw a wobbler"
CONSTRUCTION	road works
COOKIE	biscuit (sweet)
COOKOUT	barbeque
CORNSTARCH	corn flour
COT	camp bed
COTTON CANDY	candy floss

47

USA	UK
COUCH POTATO	T.V. addict, inactive person
COUNT OFF	lose marks
COVER CHARGE	entrance fee
CRACKER	biscuit (unsweetened)
CRAZY BONE	funny bone
CREAM OF WHEAT	semolina
CREEK	stream
CRULLER	small doughnut/cake
CRY UNCLE	admit default
CUFFS (on pants)	turnups (on trousers)
CUPBOARD	kitchen cabinet
CUSTOM-MADE	bespoke, made to measure
CUTE	attractive, quaint
CUT THE MUSTARD	meet required standard
CUTTING IN LINE	queue jumping

D

DAVENPORT	large sofa
DEAD TO RIGHTS	red-handed
DEALERSHIP	garage with car manufacturer's franchise
DECK (cards)	pack
DEEP SIX	get rid of
DELI	delicatessen shop
DENATURED ALCOHOL	methylated spirits/meths
DERBY HAT	bowler hat

USA	UK
DETOUR	diversion
DIAPER	nappy
DICTY	stylish
DIDDLY-SQUAT	nothing
DIDO	prank, caper
DIME STORE	inexpensive multi-goods store
DINKY	trifling
DISHTOWEL	tea towel
DIVIDED HIGHWAY	dual carriageway
DOCKET	list of court cases
DOG'S AGE	donkey's years
DOOHICKEY	small object
DOWNTOWN	town centre, city centre
DRAFT (THE)	conscription
DRAPES	curtains
DRESSER	chest of drawers
DRUGSTORE	chemist shop
DRY GOODS STORE	drapery
DUCK SOUP	easy task, money for jam
DUMMY UP	keep quiet
DUMPSTER	skip
DUPLEX	semi-detached property

USA	UK

E

EAT CROW	submit to humiliation
EDITORIAL	leader
EFFICIENCY	self-catering apartment
EGGPLANT	aubergine
ELECTRIC CORD	flex
ELEVATOR	lift
ENGLISH MUFFIN	type of crumpet
ENTREE	main course of meal

F

FACULTY	staff
FAIR-HAIRED BOY	blue-eyed boy
FALL	autumn
FAUCET	tap
FEEB	stupid person, idiot
FEISTY	aggressive
FENDER	bumper (car), mudguard (bike)
FIELD HOCKEY	hockey
FINK	nasty person, telltale
FIRST BALCONY	upper circle
FIRST FLOOR	ground floor
FIXINGS	meal accompaniments, trimmings

USA	UK
FLACK	publicity agent
FLASHLIGHT	torch
FLAT PAINT	emulsion
FLIVVER	cheap car or aeroplane
FLOOR LAMP	standard lamp
FLOP HOUSE	doss house
FLUB	botch, bungle
FLUBDUB	claptrap, bombastic language
FLUID OUNCE (U.S.)	1.041 U.K. fluid ounces
FLUNK	fail
FLYER	leaflet
FOOSBALL	table soccer
FREE SHIPPING	carriage paid
FREEWAY	motorway
FREIGHT/FREIGHT TRUCK	goods/goods wagon
FRENCH FRIES	chips
FRESHMAN	first year undergraduate
FRIGATE	large destroyer
FRITZ (ON THE)	out of order
FRONT DESK	reception
FUN FAIR	school or church bazaar
FUNK	strong smell

G

GABFEST	long spell of talking
GAINER (FULL)	somersault
GALLON (U.S.)	0.833 U.K. gallon
GARAGE SALE	house clearance sale
GARBAGE	rubbish
GARBAGE TRUCK/CAN	dustcart/bin
GARTER BELT	suspender belt
GARTERS	suspenders
GAS/GASOLINE	petrol
GAS STATION	petrol/filling station
GEAR/STICK SHIFT	gear lever
GET ON THE STICK	take hold of the situation
GIZMO	gadget
GOLDBRICK	shirker, lazy person
GOOF OFF	skive
GOOSE EGG (sports)	duck, no score
G.O.P.	Grand Old Party (Republican)
GOUGE	swindle, cheat
GRAB BAG	lucky dip
GRADE	class, form, year
GRADE CROSSING	level crossing
GRADE/GRAMMAR SCHOOL	junior school
GRANDSTANDING	playing to the gallery
GREENBACK	U. S. banknote
GRIDIRON	American football or the field
GRINDER	hardworking student, type of sandwich

USA	UK
GRIPSACK	travelling bag/suitcase
GROSS	horrible, foul
GROUND/GROUND WIRE	earth/earthwire
GROUND BEEF	minced beef
GRUBSTAKE	investment in new enter-prise, expecting a share of profits
GULCH	ravine, gully
GUMBO	spicy soup made with okra
GUMSHOE	galosh, detective

H

HABERDASHERY	a men's clothing and furnishings shop
HALF STAFF	half-mast
HAMBURGER BUN	bap
HAMBURGER MEAT	minced beef
HAND OFF (sports)	to hand the ball to a teammate
HAPPENSTANCE	thing that happens by chance
HARD CANDY	boiled sweets
HARDSCRABBLE	minimum return from maximum effort
HARDWARE STORE	ironmongers
HARVESTMAN	daddy longlegs
HASH-SLINGER	waiter/waitress

USA	UK
HATCHECK PERSON	cloakroom attendant
HAUL/HAUL ASS	to go fast
HAZING	bullying, humiliating
HEAD	toilet
HEADCHEESE	potted meat
HEAD/VALVE JOB (automotive)	decoke
HEATER	handgun/firearm
HEINIE	bum, buttocks
HEIST	robbery
HELLION	mischievious, troublesome, usually a child
HICK	country bumpkin
HICKEY	love bite, also a pipe bender
HIGH BALL	whiskey and water with ice
HIGHBINDER	swindler or ruffian
HIGH BOY	tall boy
HIGH-MUCK-A-MUCK	Lord muck
HIKE	raise
HOBO	tramp or wanderer
HOCK/IN HOCK	pawn/in debt
HOCKEY	ice hockey
HOG CHOLERA	swine fever
HOG PEN	pig sty
HOKEY	corny
HOMELY (person)	ugly, unattractive
HOMEMAKER	housewife
HOMER	home run in baseball
HOOCH	alcoholic drink, usually illicit
HOOD (auto)	bonnet

USA	UK
HOOKY (play)	truant
HOOSEGOW	prison
HOOTERS	breasts
HOPE CHEST	bottom drawer
HORSE OPERA	western film
HOT DOG BUN	bridge roll
HUNDREDWEIGHT	100 pounds
HUSH PUPPY	quick-fried maize bread
HUTCH	Welsh dresser

I

ICEBOX	refrigerator
INCORPORATED/INC.	Limited/Ltd.
INFORMATION (phone)	directory enquiries
INNERSPRING	interior sprung
INSTALLMENT PLAN	hire purchase
INTERMISSION	interval
INTERN	medical graduate, advanced student
INTERSECTION	road junction

J

USA	UK
JACKHAMMER	pneumatic hammer
JACKRABBIT	hare
JAW BREAKER	gob stopper
JELLO	jelly
JELLY ROLL	Swiss roll
JIBE (nautical)	tack
JIBE	agree with, fit in with
JIGGER	tot
JIMMY	jemmy
JITNEY	small bus, jeep
JIVE	tease, fool; meaningless talk
JOCK	athletic male
JOHN DOE	Joe Bloggs
JOHN HENRY/HANCOCK	person's signature
JOHNNY-JUMP-UP	violet/pansy
JUMBLE	small circular sweet-cake
JUMP ROPE	skip rope

K

USA	UK
KAFFEE KLATSCH	coffee morning, informal gathering
KEDS	plimsolls
KEGLER	bowler, skittle player

56

USA	UK
KEROSINE/KEROSENE	paraffin
KNICKERS	plus fours
KNOCK UP	make pregnant
KOOK	crazy or eccentric person

L

USA	UK
LADYBUG	ladybird
LADYFINGER	small finger-shaped sponge cake
LAID OFF	made redundant
LALLYGAG	to loiter
LAP ROBE	travelling rug
LAWN BOWLING	green bowling
LEASE	let
LEASH	lead
LEERY	wary
LEGAL HOLIDAY	bank holiday
LICENSE PLATE	vehicle number plate
LIGHTNING BUG	firefly
LIMA BEAN	broad bean
LINE (stand in)	queue (up)
LINE UP	identification parade
LIP SYNCH	mime to recorded music
LIQUOR	spirits
LIQUOR STORE	off licence
LIVERWURST	liver sausage

USA	UK
LOADED FOR BEAR	fully prepared
LOAN SHARK	one who charges interest at an unlawful rate
LOBBY	foyer
LOCATE	settle down with home or business
LOCATOR	one who determines land boundaries when disputed
LOCOMOTIVE ENGINEER	train driver
LOGE	front dress circle
LOGGER	lumberjack
LOGY	sluggish, lethargic
LONG DOZEN	baker's dozen (13)
LONG GREEN	paper money
LOVE SEAT	settee, usually a two-seater
LUMBER	unwanted household goods
LUMBER ROOM	box room
LUMMOX	clumsy person
LUSH	an alcoholic

M

MACKINAW	a warm, belted cloth coat
MAIL	post
MAIL CARRIER /MAILMAN	postal carrier/postman
MAIL DROP	pillar box
MAIN STEM	main street

USA	UK
MAJOR LEAGUE	principal league in professional baseball
MALL (SHOPPING)	precinct/arcade
MASON JAR	Killner jar
MEAT GRINDER	mincer
MEDIAN	central reservation
MEDICAID	government sponsored medical aid for the needy
MEDICARE	government insurance program providing medical care for the elderly
MELD	to blend, combine, mix
MESA	a high, steep-sided, rocky plateau
MEZZANINE	dress circle
MICHIGAN (card game)	Newmarket
MINOR LEAGUE	other than the principal (major) league in baseball
MOLASSES	black treacle
MONEY ORDER	postal order
MONKEY WRENCH	adjustable spanner
MOONSHINE	illicit liquor
MORTICIAN	undertaker
MOTHER'S DAY	second Sunday in May
MOVIES	pictures, films
MOXIE	courage, daring, energy
MUFFIN	bun

USA	UK
MUFFLER (auto)	silencer
MUGWUMP	one who "sits on the fence"
MULLIGAN	a meat and vegetable stew
MUTUAL FUND	unit trust

N

NATATORIUM	indoor swimming pool
NEWSDEALER/NEWSTAND	newsagent
NEWSHAWK/NEWSHOUND	reporter
NICKELODEON	early jukebox
NIGHTSTICK	truncheon
NIGHT TABLE	bedside table
911	999
NIPPLE (on baby bottle)	teat
NONPAREIL	hundreds and thousands
NOTARIZE	attest as a notary
NOT HAY	a lot of money
NOTIONS STORE	haberdashery
NUKE IT	cook in a microwave oven

O

USA	UK
OFF-COLOR	somewhat indecent
OFFICE (doctor's)	surgery
OFF THE RACK	off the peg
OFF THE WALL	bizarre, strange
OIL PAN	sump
ONE WAY TICKET	single ticket
ON TAP (beer)	draught
ON THE LAM	running away
ON THE NOSE	precisely
ORCHESTRA SEATS	stalls
ORNERY	unpleasant, cantankerous
OUTLET	power point
OUTLET PLUG	mains lead
OUT OF WHACK	out of order
OVERPASS	fly over

P

USA	UK
PACIFIER	dummy
PACKAGE	parcel
PACKAGE STORE	off license
PADDLE (ping pong)	bat (table tennis)
PALOOKA	lout, poor performer at sport

USA	UK
PANHANDLE	to beg in the street
PANHANDLE	narrow projecting strip of land, such as the Texas panhandle
PANTIHOSE	tights
PANTYWAIST	nancy boy, effeminate man
PAP SMEAR	cervical smear
PARKING LOT	car park
PARTICLE BOARD	chip board
PASS (vehicle)	overtake
PATSY	scapegoat, victimised or deceived person
PAVEMENT	roadway
PEEPER	private detective
PENITENTIARY	prison
PEPPER SHAKER	pepper pot
PHI BETA KAPPA	member of the oldest college fraternity
PICKY	fussy, finicky
PINCH HITTER	substitute
PINKSTER	Whitsuntide
PINOCHLE	card game with double pack pronounced "P nuckle" (9s to aces only)
PINOLE	flour made from parched cornflour
PINTO	piebald horse
PIT	stone of a fruit
PITCHER	jug
PITMAN (mechanical)	connecting rod
PLACE BET	horse to be first or second
PLUG UGLY	ruffian, gangster
PODIATRIST	chiropodist

USA	UK
POLICE CAPTAIN	police inspector
POLLIWOG	tadpole
PONDEROSA	pine tree
PONY CAR	sporty two-door car, e.g., Mustang or Pinto
POPSICLE	iced lolly
POSTAGE METER	franking machine
POT CHEESE	cottage cheese
POT HOLDERS/GLOVES	oven cloth/gloves
POWDERED SUGAR	icing sugar
PRAIRIE SCHOONER	large covered wagon
PRECINCT	district
PREVIEW (movies)	trailer
PRINCIPAL	headmaster/mistress
PRIVATE SCHOOL	public school
PROCTOR	invigilator
PROM	school dance
PUBLIC SCHOOL	school managed by public authorities
PUMP	ladies court shoe
PURSE	handbag
PX (post exchange)	NAAFI

USA	UK

Q

QUAHOG	edible clam
QUARTER DAYS	Jan. 1, Apr. 1, Jul. 1, Oct. 1
QUARTER HORSE	horse bred to run strongly over the quartermile
QUARTER NOTE	crotchet
QUIRT	riding crop
QUONSET HUT	Nissen hut

R

RAILROAD TIES	railway sleepers
RAIN CHECK	postponement
RAMP	slip road
RANGE	cooker
RANGER	warden patrolling park or forest areas
RATTLER	goods train; rattlesnake
RAZZ	tease, deride
REALTOR	estate agent
REALTY	real estate
RECAP (tire)	retread
RECESS (school)	break
RESTROOM	toilet/W.C.
RESUMÉ	C.V.

USA	UK
RHINESTONE	diamante
RHUBARB	expression for a heated dispute
RIFFED	sacked, made redundant
RINKY DINK	old fashioned, delapidated
ROACH	cockroach
ROMAINE LETTUCE	cos lettuce
ROOKIE	new team member
ROOT BEER	soda pop made from plant root extracts
ROUGH RIDER	person who breaks in horses
ROUND TRIP	return
ROUSTABOUT	unskilled labourer, especially on the docks or oil rigs
ROWEN	aftermath, field of stubble
ROW HOUSE	terraced house
RUBBING ALCOHOL	surgical spirit
RUBE	yokel
RUMBLE SEAT	dickey seat
RUMPUS ROOM	games room
RUTABAGA	swede

S

SAD SACK	very inept person
SALES CLERK	shop assitant

USA	UK
SALUTATORIAN	second ranking member of a graduating class who delivers opening speech at graduation
SAND DOLLAR	round flat sea urchin
SASHAY	walk ostentatiously or casually
SCADS	large quantities, lashings
SCALPER	ticket tout
SCAM	rip off
SCHEDULE	time table
SCHLEMIEL	foolish or unlucky person
SCHLOCH	poor quality; secondhand
SCOPE OUT	check into, investigate
SCOTCH TAPE	Sellotape
SCRAPPLE	stewed meat and flour pressed into cakes
SCRATCH PAD	scribbling pad
SCREEN	window/door netting, allowing air through, but not insects
SCREWBALL	strange or crazy person
SCROD	young cod
SECOND FLOOR	first floor
SECOND GUESS	know by hindsight
SECOND STOREY MAN	cat burglar
SEDAN	family car, saloon car
SEMESTER (school)	term
SEND UP	put in prison
SHAKE DOWN	extort money from; a raid
SHARK	outstanding student
SHAVE TAIL	mule just broken in
SHEERS	net curtains

USA	UK
SHILL	person used as a decoy
SHIPPING	postage
SHIRT WAIST	blouse
SHOAT	piglet
SHOO FLY	temporary road or railway; guard detailed to watch people
SHOO FLY PIE	sweet treacle dessert
SHOO IN	a certainty
SHOTS	jabs, inoculations
SHOWER	party for giving presents to a prospective bride or expectant mother
SHREDDED (coconut)	desiccated
SHUCK	remove oysters/shellfish from shells
SIDEWALK	pavement
SIDING	a building's exterior cladding
SIGNAL TOWER	signal box
SKID ROW	part of town frequented by vagrants, alcoholics, etc.
SKIN GAME	swindling game, confidence trick
SKIVVIES	underwear
SLATE	schedule; nominate
SLEW	a large number, many
SLICKER	a plausible rogue
SLINGSHOT	catapult
SLIP COVER	loose cover
SNAP	easy task
SNAPS	press studs
SNEAKERS	plimsolls, gym shoes

USA	UK
SNOLLYGOSTER	shrewd, unscrupulous person
SNOW JOB	attempt to persuade by misleading talk
SOCKDOLOGER	decisive blow
SODA	pop, soda pop
SODA CRACKER	cream cracker
SOLITAIRE (cards)	patience
SOPHOMORE	second year at high school or undergraduate
SPELUNKER	pot holer
SPIEL	glib or persuasive speech
SQUASH	marrow
STAKE OUT	to place under surveillance
STANDPATTER	one opposed to change, traditiona
STAND THE GAFF	endure hardship
STATION WAGON	estate car
STEAL (A)	a bargain; easy task
STICK SHIFT	gear lever/stick
STOGY	long cigar
STOOL PIGEON	copper's nark
STREETCAR	tram
STRING BEAN	runner bean
STROLLER	push chair
STUDIO APT.	a bedsit
SUBDIVISION	housing estate
SUBWAY	tube, underground
SUCKER	toffy lolly
SURF & TURF	a beef and seafood meal
SUSPENDERS	braces
SWAN DIVE	swallow dive

USA	UK
SWITCHBACK	road with alternating left and right bends
SWITCHBLADE	flick knife

T

USA	UK
TAD	small amount, small boy
TAFFY	a kind of toffee
TAG	motor vehicle license plate
TAG DAY	flag day
TALK TURKEY	be straightforward
TAR HEEL	native of North Carolina
TEAMSTER	lorry driver
TEETER-TOTTER	seesaw
TEMBLOR	earthquake
TEXAS GATE	cattle grid
THUMB TACK	drawing pin
TICK-TACK-TOE	noughts and crosses
TILT A WHIRL	waltzer
TOTAL (vehicle)	write off
TOUCH BASE	contact, get in touch with
TRACTOR TRAILER	articulated lorry
TRAFFIC CIRCLE	roundabout
TRAILER	caravan
TRAILER PARK	caravan site
TRASH CAN	dustbin
TRUCK FARM	market garden

USA	UK
TRUCK STOP	transport cafe
TRUNK (car)	boot
TUCKERED OUT	tired out, knackered
TURRET LATHE	capstan lathe
TURTLENECK	poloneck
TUXEDO/TUX	dinner jacket
TWO BIT	petty, small time
TWO BITS	25 cents

U

USA	UK
UNDERGRADUATES	
FRESHMAN	1st year
SOPHOMORE	2nd year
JUNIOR	3rd year
SENIOR	4th year
UP CHUCK	vomit

V

USA	UK
VALANCE	pelmet
VALEDICTORIAN	highest ranking student in a graduating class who gives farewell speech at graduation
VEST	waistcoat

70

USA	UK
VETERAN	ex-serviceman
VETERANS' DAY	Remembrance Day

W

WALKING PAPERS	marching orders, dismissal
WASH CLOTH	face flannel
WASH UP	wash hands and face
WAVE (Women's navy)	WREN
WAY STATION	minor railway station, a halt
WET BACK	illegal immigrant from Mexico
WHAMMY	hex, setback, shocking blow
WHISTLE-STOP	minor railway station, a halt
WHOLE NOTE	semibreve
WICKET	small sliding window or opening (e.g., at a ticket office)
WIND BREAKER	wind cheater
WINGDING	wild party
WRECKER	breakdown lorry
WRIST PIN	gudgeon pin

USA	UK

Y

YARD	garden of a house
YARD SALE	house clearance sale
YAWP	to cry out; to talk continually and noisily
YEGG	burglar, safecracker
YELLOW DOG	mongrel; someone anti-union
Y'ALL (YOU ALL)	you

Z

ZEE	z
ZILCH	nothing
ZINGER	sharp witticism
ZIP	nil, no score
ZIP CODE	postal code
ZUCCHINI	courgette

BIRDS COMMON TO EUROPE AND NORTH AMERICA

SCIENTIFIC NAME

UK

USA

Gavia stellata

Red-throated
Diver

Red-throated
Loon

Gavia immer

Great Northern
Diver

Common Loon

Gavia adamsii

White-billed
Diver

Yellow-billed
Loon

Gavia arctica

Black-throated
Diver

Arctic Loon

Podiceps auritus

Slavonian Grebe

Horned Grebe

Podiceps Nigricollis

Black-necked
Grebe

Eared Grebe

Oceanodromo Castro

Madeiran Petrel

Band-rumped
Storm Petrel

73

UK		USA
	Nycticorax Nycticorax	
Night Heron		Black-crowned Night Heron
	Cygnus Columbianus	
Bewick's Swan		Tundra Swan
	Branta bernicla	
Brent Goose		Brant
	Clangula hyemalis	
Long-tailed Duck		Oldsquaw
	Melanitta fusca	
Velvet Scoter		White-winged Scoter
	Melanitta nigra	
Common Scoter		Black Scoter
	Mergus merganser	
Goosander		Common Merganser
	Aegypius monachus	
Black Vulture		
	Coragyps atratus	
		Black Vulture

UK		USA
	Buteo lagopus	
Rough-legged Buzzard		Rough-legged Hawk
	Circus cyaneus	
Hen Harrier		Northern Harrier
	Lagopus Lagopus	
Willow/Red Grouse		Willow Ptarmigan
	Lagopus mutus	
Ptarmigan		Rock Ptarmigan
	Charradrius alexandrinas	
Kentish Plover		Snowy Plover
	Pluvialis squatarolis	
Grey Plover		Black-bellied Plover
	Arenaria interpres	
Turnstone		Ruddy Turnstone
	Calidris canutus	
Knot		Red Knot

UK		USA
	Phalaropus fulicarius	
Grey Phalarope		Red Phalarope
	Stercorarius parasiticus	
Arctic Skua		Parasitic Jaeger
	Larus canus	
Common Gull		Mew Gull
	Uria aalge	
Guillemot		Common Murre
	Uria lomvia	
Brunnich's Guillemot		Thick-billed Murre
	Alle alle	
Little Auk		Dovekie
	Aegolius funereus	
Tengmalm's Owl		Boreal Owl
	Hirundo rustica	
Swallow		Barn Swallow
	Eremophilia alpestris	
Shore Lark		Horned Lark

UK		USA
	Riparia riparia	
Sand Martin		Bank Swallow
	Pica pica	
Magpie		Black-billed Magpie
	Troglodytes troglodytes	
Wren		Winter Wren
	Bombycilla garrulus	
Waxwing		Bohemian Waxwing
	Lanius excubitor	
Great Grey Shrike		Northern Shrike
	Carduelis hornemanni	
Arctic Redpoll		Hoary Redpoll

NOTES

TEMPERATURE CONVERSIONS

Degrees F (Farenheit) to Degrees C (Celsius/Centigrade)

Take Farenheit temperature, subtract 32 degrees and multiply by 5/9; or take the Centigrade temperature, multiply by 9/5 and add 32 degrees.

Degrees F	=	Degrees C
104	=	40
98.6	=	37
95	=	35
86	=	30
77	=	25
68	=	20
59	=	15
50	=	10
41	=	5
32	=	0
23	=	-5
14	=	-10
5	=	-15
0	=	-18
-9	=	-23
-18	=	-28
-40	=	-40

NOTES

U.K. TO U.S.A. COMPARISON MEASURES

Imperial pint	=	approximately 20 fluid ounces
U.S. pint	=	16 fluid ounces
Imperial gallon	=	approximately 157 fluid ounces
U.S. gallon	=	128 fluid ounces
U.K. Hundred weight	=	112 pounds
U.S. Hundred weight	=	100 pounds

To further complicate the issue, the U.K. fluid ounce varies slightly from the U.S. fluid ounce.

The U.S. gallon = approximately 4/5 U.K. gallon, or the U.K. gallon = 1 1/4 times the U.S. gallon.

NOTE: In the U.K. people express their weight in "stones." A "stone" is equal to 14 pounds.

U.K. TO U.S.A. COMPARATIVE SIZES

Since clothing and shoes may vary, comparisons are only approximate. Generally U.K. shoe sizes are 1 to 1 1/2 sizes lower than U.S. sizes (Men's 9 in the U.K. is 10 in the U.S., Women's size 6 U.K. is about 7 1/2 U.S.). Women's dresses may run 2 sizes lower in the U.S. (14 U.K. is 12 U.S.). Metric sizes are also used, and they may become more prominent as standards of the European community are established.

ELECTRICITY

U.K.	U.S.
240 volts, A.C. 50 cycles.	120 volts, 60 cycles.

EMERGENCIES

U.K. - Dial 999. U.S. - Dial 911 or O for the Operator.

SOLITAIRE PUBLISHING

P.O. Box 14508   Tampa, Florida 33690   (813) 876-0286

THANK YOU!

FOR HAVING PURCHASED THE U.K. TO U.S.A. DICTIONARY.

If your company or organization would like to order
a quantity of The U.K. to U.S.A. Dictionary,
contact us for discounts.

If you would like to order a single copy for a
friend or associate, please complete the form below.

For U.S addresses, enclose a check/money order for
$7.95. International addresses, please enclose a
money order for $13.95 USD. FL residents - add 6.5%
sales tax.

Name_____

Address_____

City, State/Country_____

Zip/Postal code_____Phone_____

___PLEASE MAIL SOLITAIRE PUBLISHING'S COMPLETE CATALOG.

We also welcome any comments or suggestions!
Mail to the address shown above.